KIM SCHAEFER

cozy
modern
quilts

23 Easy Pieced Projects to Bust Your Stash

C&T PUBLISHING

- Publisher: **Amy Marson**
- Creative Director: **Gailen Runge**
- Acquisitions Editor: **Susanne Woods**
- Editor: **Lynn Koolish**
- Technical Editors: **Helen Frost** and **Susan Nelson**
- Copyeditor/Proofreader: **Wordfirm Inc.**

- Cover/Book Designer: **Kristen Yenche**
- Production Coordinator: **Zinnia Heinzmann**
- Production Editor: **Julia Cianci**
- Illustrator: **Tim Manibusan**
- Photography by **Christina Carty-Francis** and **Diane Pedersen** of C&T Publishing, Inc., unless otherwise noted.

Library of Congress Cataloging-in-Publication Data

Schaefer, Kim, 1960-

Cozy modern quilts : 23 easy pieced projects to bust your stash / Kim Schaefer.

  p. cm.

ISBN 978-1-57120-622-0 (soft cover)

1. Patchwork--Patterns. 2. Machine quilting--Patterns. 3. Household linens. I. Title.

TT835.S2827 2009

746.46'041--dc22

2009011155

Printed in China

10 9 8 7 6 5 4

dedication

To quilters everywhere, especially the beginners, this book is for you!

acknowledgments

Thank you to:

The entire staff at C&T Publishing. I am honored to work with such a creative and talented team.

Diane Minkley for the beautiful longarm quilting on every project in this book.

Julie Karasek and the staff at Patched Works, Inc., for not running and hiding when I walk in the door to have my ¼ yard scraps cut from zillions of bolts of fabric

My husband, Gary Schaefer, for everything, but especially for learning to use a rotary cutter, ruler, and mat to cut the remaining fabric on the last quilt for this book after I cut my hand on a rotary blade (ouch!).

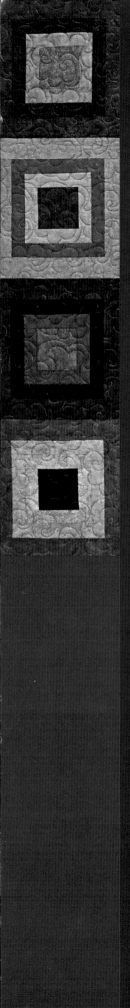

contents

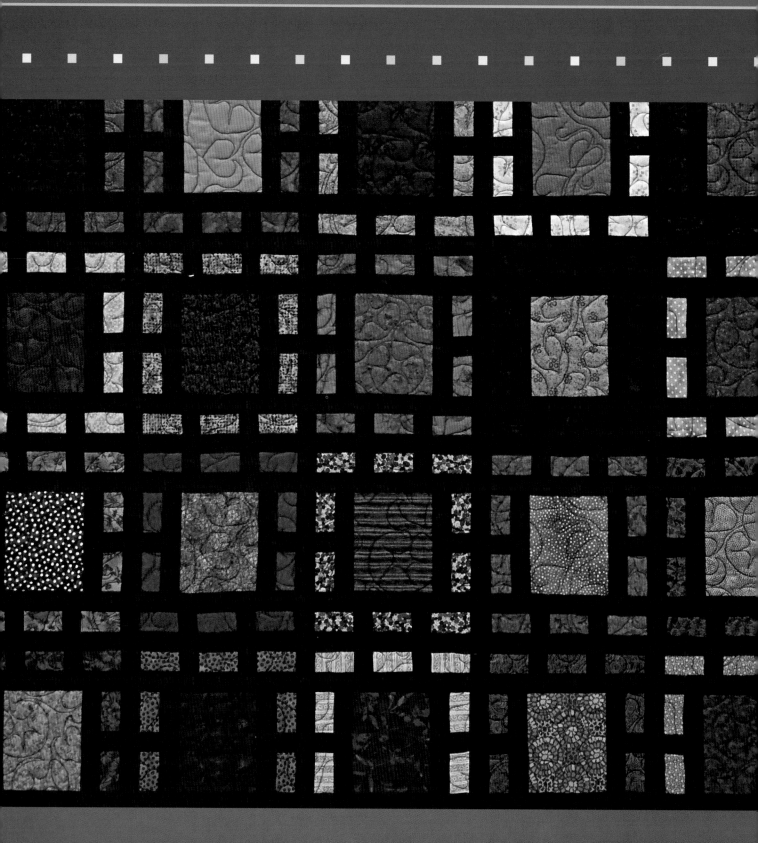

introduction

In this book, you will find a collection of scrappy, pieced projects to decorate your home. There are lap quilts, wall quilts, table runners, and placemats. All of the projects are made from just two simple shapes—the square and the rectangle—with no tricky measurements or stretchy bias edges. Whether you are a beginning or a seasoned quilter who wants something quick and easy, there are projects suitable for your skill level.

Although I am known best for my appliqué designs, I started out doing pieced quilts, which I still love. Piecing is really the foundation of all quilt-making, an integral building block to more advanced skills.

The designs are basic and very versatile. The patterns adapt easily to your style preference, whether it be classic and traditional or more contemporary. Your color and fabric choices will determine your particular style. Most of my quilts are very scrappy; in general, the more fabrics I use, the more I like the quilt. Although the quilts are scrappy, they are not completely unplanned. Many of the quilts offer a great opportunity to utilize your stash. However, I must confess—I do buy "scraps." If I don't have enough of what I want for a particular project, I buy it.

general directions

rotary cutting

I recommend that you use a rotary cutter, an acrylic ruler, and a cutting mat to cut all the fabrics used in the pieced blocks, borders, and bindings. Trim the blocks and borders with these tools as well.

piecing

All piecing measurements include ¼" seam allowances. If you sew an accurate ¼" seam, you will succeed! My biggest and best quiltmaking tip is to learn to sew an accurate ¼" seam.

pressing

Press seams to one side, preferably toward the darker fabric. Press flat, and avoid sliding the iron over the pieces, which could distort and stretch them. When you join two seamed sections, press the seams in opposite directions so you can nest the seams and reduce bulk.

putting it all together

When all the blocks for a project are completed, lay them out on the floor or, if you are lucky enough to have one, a design wall. Arrange and rearrange the blocks until you are happy with the overall look. Each project has specific directions as well as diagrams and photos for assembly.

borders

If the quilt borders need to be longer than 40", join cross-wise strips of fabric at a 45° angle as necessary, and cut the strips to the desired length. All borders in the book are straight cut; no mitered corners.

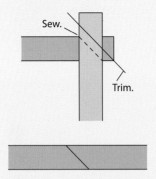

Join borders with 45° angle.

layering the quilt

Cut the batting and backing pieces 4" to 5" larger than the quilt top. Place the pressed backing on the bottom, right side down. Place the batting over the backing, and place the quilt top on top, right side up. Make sure all the layers are flat and smooth and the quilt top is centered over the batting and backing. Pin or baste the quilt.

note

If you are going to have your top quilted by a long-arm quilter, contact the quilter for specific batting and backing requirements, as those requirements may differ from the instructions above.

Since I prefer not to piece the backing for the table runners, the fabric amounts allow for the length of the runner. I add the leftover fabric to my stash.

quilting

Quilting is a personal choice—you may prefer either hand or machine quilting. My favorite method is to send the quilt top to a longarm quilter. This method keeps my number of unfinished tops low and the number of finished quilts high.

color and fabric choices

All the projects in this book are made using 100% cotton fabrics. I find they are easy to work with and readily available at any local quilt shop.

I have used both traditional and contemporary color choices for the quilts and other projects. I have a very relaxed approach to color and tend to make my quilts very scrappy. As I've said, the more fabrics I use, the more I like the quilt. The overall feel of a quilt can be changed dramatically by color choice, especially in pieced quilts. The *Tic-Tac Wall Quilt* (page 32) is the same block design as the *Color Splash Table Runner* (page 50), yet the fabric choices for each make them look very different. The *Blueberries and Butterscotch Wall Quilt* (page 40) has a very traditional look, while the *Pastel Picnic Table Runner* on (page 53), which uses the same block, has a fresh, spring-like look.

Thankfully everyone has different tastes when it comes to color. Whether you prefer traditional, contemporary, or something in between, any of the designs can be adapted to your preference.

make the quilt your own

If you want to change the size of a quilt, simply add or subtract blocks or change the width of the borders. Many times, eliminating a border will give the quilt a more modern, contemporary look. Your color choices may be totally different from mine.

yardage and fabric requirements

I have given yardage and fabric requirements for each project, with many calling for a total amount of assorted fabrics that can be used as a base for your quilt. The yardage amounts may vary depending on several factors, such as the size of the quilt, the number of fabrics used, and the number of pieces you cut from each fabric.

Binding fabric amounts allow for 2"-wide strips cut on the straight of grain. I usually use the same fabric for backing and binding; it's a good way to use leftover backing.

projects

Quilted by Diane Minkley

merry go round lap quilt

FINISHED BLOCK SIZES: 10″ × 10″, 5″ × 5″ ■ FINISHED LAP QUILT: 79½″ × 79½″

Rich, textured solids in a variety of colors make this quilt lusciously
vibrant. The pieced border frames the quilt top for a traditional
look. Leave off the border for a more modern-looking quilt top.

materials

- 4¼ yards total assorted brights for pieced blocks
- ¾ yard teal for inner border
- 1¾ yards total assorted brights for pieced border blocks
- 1⅛ yards brown for lattice in pieced border
- 7¼ yards backing and binding
- 84" × 84" batting

cutting

Cut from the assorted brights for the pieced blocks:

    36 squares 3½" × 3½"

    72 rectangles 1½" × 3½"

    144 rectangles 1½" × 5½"

    72 rectangles 1½" × 7½"

    72 rectangles 2" × 7½"

    72 rectangles 2" × 10½"

Cut from the teal for the inner border:

    2 strips 3" × 60½" for the side borders*

    2 strips 3" × 65½" for the top and bottom borders*

    Cut 7 strips 3" × fabric width, piece the strips end to end (see page 9), and cut the border pieces.

Cut from the assorted brights for the pieced border blocks:

    144 squares 1½" × 1½"

    192 rectangles 1½" × 3½"

    96 rectangles 1½" × 5½"

Cut from the brown for the lattice in the border:

    48 rectangles 1½" × 5½"

    4 strips 1½" × 65½"*

    4 strips 1½" × 79½"*

    Cut 15 strips 1½" × fabric width, piece the strips end to end (see page 9), and cut the lattice pieces.

piecing

Piece the block as shown. Press. Make 36 blocks.

Step 1

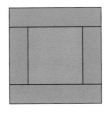

Step 2

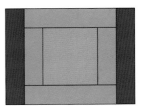

Step 3

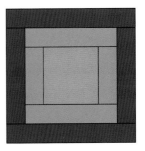

Step 4

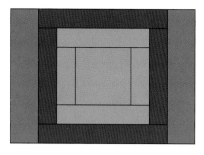

Step 5

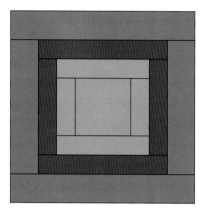

Step 6

putting it all together

QUILT CENTER

1. Arrange and sew together the blocks in 6 rows of 6 blocks each. Press.

2. Sew together the rows. Press.

INNER BORDER

1. Sew the 2 side borders to the quilt top. Press toward the borders.

2. Sew the top and bottom borders to the quilt top. Press toward the borders.

PIECED BORDER

1. Piece the block as shown. Press. Make 48 blocks.

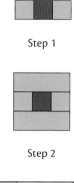

Step 1

Step 2

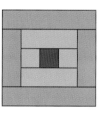

Step 3

Step 4

2. Arrange and sew together 2 rows of 11 blocks and 10 lattice pieces 1½″ × 5½″ to make the side borders. Press.

3. Sew the 1½″ × 65½″ lattice pieces to the sides of each border.

4. Sew the 2 side borders to the quilt top. Press.

5. Arrange and sew together 2 rows of 13 blocks and 14 lattice pieces 1½″ × 5½″ to make the top and bottom borders. Press.

6. Sew the 1½″ × 79½″ lattice pieces to the sides of each border. Press.

7. Sew the top and bottom borders to the quilt top. Press.

finishing

1. Layer the quilt top with batting and backing. Baste or pin.

2. Quilt as desired and bind.

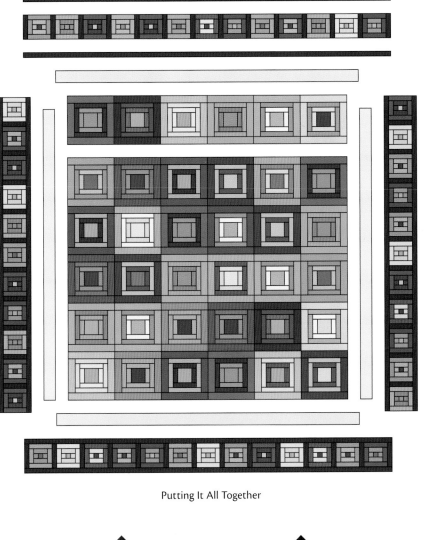

Putting It All Together

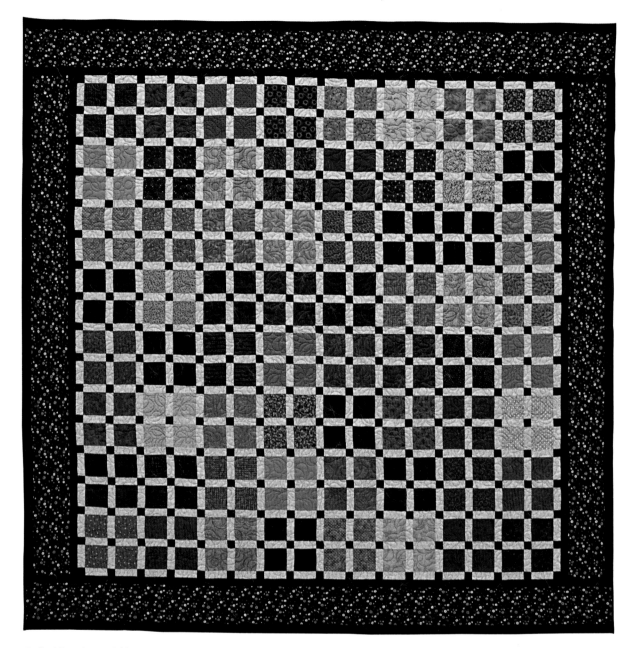

Quilted by Diane Minkley

connect four lap quilt

FINISHED BLOCK SIZE: 3″ × 3″ ■ **FINISHED LAP QUILT: 79½″ × 79½″**

Place the fabrics to create sections of four squares connected with
lattice, then sew this scrappy lap quilt together in rows. The dark
border fabric frames the quilt top for a more traditional look.

materials

- 2¾ yards total assorted brights for blocks
- 2¼ yards light for lattice
- 1¼ yards black for lattice connecting squares and borders
- 1⅝ yards black dot for border
- 7¼ yards for backing and binding
- 84″ × 84″ batting

cutting

Cut 256 squares 3½″ × 3½″ from the assorted brights for the blocks.

Cut 544 rectangles 1½″ × 3½″ from the light for the lattice.

Cut from the black:

269 squares 1½″ × 1½″ for the lattice connecting squares

4 strips 1½″ × 65½″ for the side borders*

4 strips 1½″ × 79½″ for the top and bottom borders*

*Cut 15 strips 1½″ × fabric width, piece the strips end to end (see page 9), and cut the border strips.

Cut from the black dot:

2 strips 5½″ × 65½″ for the side borders*

2 strips 5½″ × 79½″ for the top and bottom borders*

*Cut 9 strips 5½″ × fabric width, piece the strips end to end (see page 9), and cut the border strips.

putting it all together

QUILT CENTER

1. Arrange the blocks into 16 rows of 16 blocks each.

2. Sew together 16 blocks and 17 lattice pieces in a row. Press. Make 16 rows.

Sew block rows; make 16.

3. Sew together 16 lattice pieces and 17 connecting squares in a row. Press. Make 17 rows.

Sew lattice rows; make 17.

4. Sew together the rows to form the quilt top. Press.

BORDERS

1. Sew 2 black strips 1½" × 65½" to 1 black dot strip 5½" × 65½" for each side border.

2. Sew the side borders to the quilt top. Press.

3. Sew 2 black strips 1½" × 79½" to 1 black dot strip 5½" × 79½" for each of the top and bottom borders. Press.

4. Sew the top and bottom borders to the quilt top. Press.

finishing

1. Layer the quilt with batting and backing. Baste or pin.

2. Quilt as desired and bind.

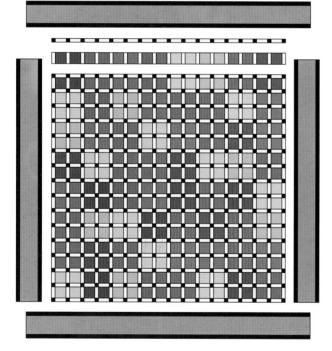

Putting It All Together

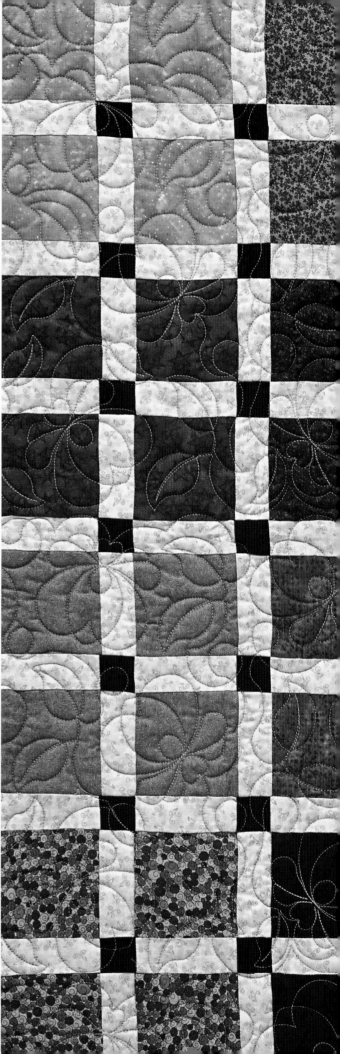

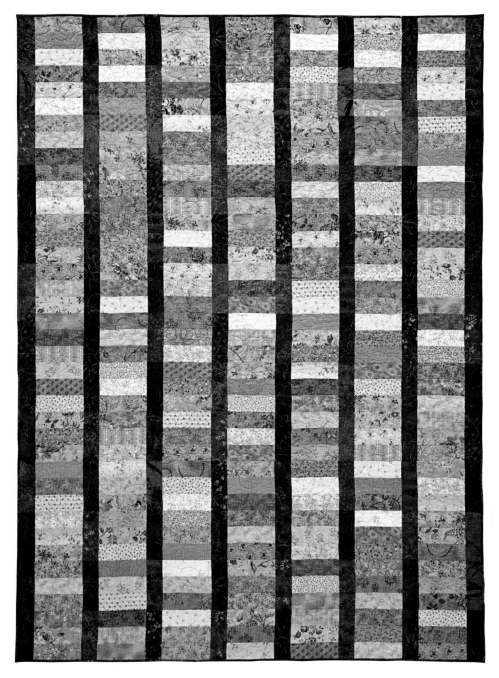

Quilted by Diane Minkley

down and across lap quilt

FINISHED BLOCK SIZE: 6″ × 6″ ■ FINISHED LAP QUILT: 58½″ × 78½″

Simple and elegant, this quilt is constructed using the same size rectangle for the entire top. Soft, serene fabrics make this quilt look as though it has been touched by the hands of time.

materials

- 3½ yards total assorted lights and mediums for pieced blocks
- 1½ yards total assorted darks for lattice

- 5¼ yards for backing and binding
- 63″ × 83″ batting

cutting

Cut 273 rectangles 2½″ × 6½″ from the assorted lights and mediums for the pieced blocks.   46 strips

Cut 104 rectangles 2½″ × 6½″ from the assorted darks for the lattice.   18 strips

piecing

Sew together 3 rectangles 2½″ × 6½″ from the assorted lights and mediums to piece the block. Press. Make 91 blocks.

Pieced blocks; make 91.

putting it all together

1. Arrange and sew together 7 blocks and 8 lattice pieces in a row. Press. Make 13 rows.

Sew lattice to blocks; make 13 rows.

2. Sew together the rows to form the quilt top. Press.

finishing

1. Layer the quilt top with batting and backing. Baste or pin.

2. Quilt as desired and bind.

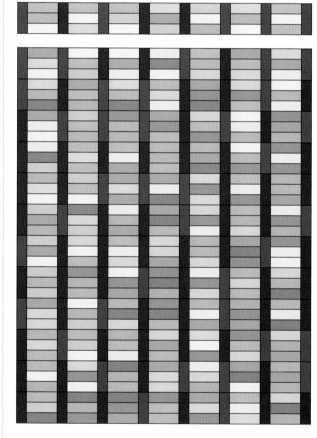

Putting It All Together

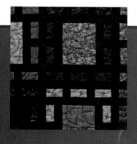

Quilted by Diane Minkley

freeze frame lap quilt

FINISHED BLOCK SIZE: 8″ × 9″ ▪ FINISHED LAP QUILT: 62½″ × 79½″

A variety of greens, purples, blues, and pinks contrasts with the black lattice to make this quilt fresh and exciting. The absence of a border gives the quilt a more modern look.

materials

- 1⅝ yards total assorted greens for pieced blocks
- 1⅝ yards total assorted purples, pinks, and blues for pieced blocks
- 3½ yards black for pieced blocks and lattice
- 5⅜ yards for backing and binding
- 67″ × 84″ batting

cutting

Cut from the assorted greens for the pieced blocks:

28 rectangles 4½″ × 5½″

280 rectangles 1½″ × 2½″

Cut from the assorted purples, pinks, and blues for the pieced blocks:

28 rectangles 4½″ × 5½″

280 rectangles 1½″ × 2½″

Cut from the black:

336 squares 1½″ × 1½″ for the pieced blocks

112 rectangles 1½″ × 5½″ for the pieced blocks

112 rectangles 1½″ × 8½″ for the pieced blocks

48 rectangles 1½″ × 9½″ for the lattice

7 strips 1½″ × 62½″ for the lattice*

Cut 12 strips 1½″ × fabric width, piece the strips end to end (see page 9), and cut the lattice pieces.

piecing

1. Piece the block as shown. Make 28 green blocks. Press.

Step 1

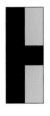

Step 2

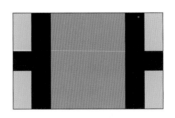

Step 3

Step 4

Step 5

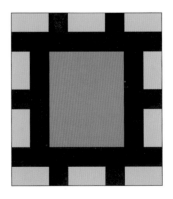

Step 6

2. Piece the block as shown. Make 28 purple, pink, or blue blocks. Press.

Step 1

Step 2

Step 3

Step 4

Step 5

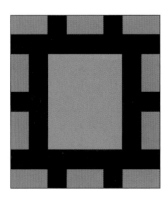

Step 6

putting it all together

1. Arrange the blocks in 8 rows of 7 blocks each.

2. Sew together 7 blocks and 6 lattice pieces 1½" × 9½" in a row. Press. Make 8 rows.

3. Sew lattice strips 1½" × 62½" between the rows to form the quilt top. Press.

finishing

1. Layer the quilt top with batting and backing. Baste or pin.

2. Quilt as desired and bind.

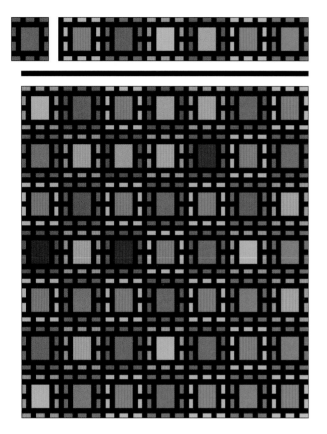

Putting It All Together

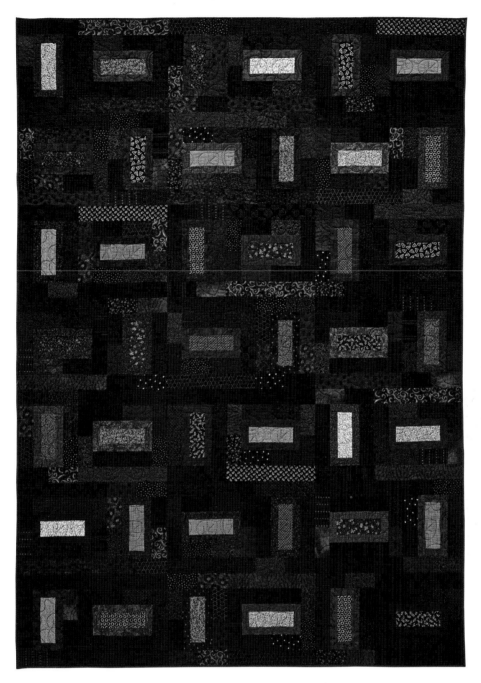

Quilted by Diane Minkley

red rover lap quilt

FINISHED BLOCK SIZES: 8″ × 12″, 12″ × 12″ ▪ FINISHED LAP QUILT: 60½″ × 84½″

Make a bold statement with graphic results, using a variety of black and red prints for this lap quilt with a contemporary twist.

materials

- ¾ yard total assorted black-and-white prints for pieced blocks
- 1¼ yards total assorted reds for pieced blocks
- 4¼ yards total assorted blacks for pieced blocks
- 5⅝ yards for backing and binding
- 65″ × 89″ batting

cutting

Cut 42 rectangles 2½″ × 6½″ from the assorted black-and-white prints for the block centers.

Cut from the assorted reds for the pieced blocks:

84 rectangles 1½″ × 6½″

84 rectangles 1½″ × 4½″

Cut from the assorted blacks for the pieced blocks:

336 rectangles 2½″ × 4½″

42 rectangles 2½″ × 12½″

piecing

1. Piece the block as shown. Press. Make 42 blocks.

Step 1

Step 2

Step 3

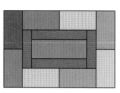

Step 4

2. Sew assorted black rectangles 2½″ × 12½″ to the top and bottom of 21 of the blocks. Press.

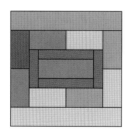

Add rectangles to 21 blocks.

putting it all together

1. Arrange and sew together the blocks in 7 rows of 6 blocks each. Press.

2. Sew together the rows to form the quilt top.

finishing

1. Layer the quilt top with batting and backing. Baste or pin.

2. Quilt as desired and bind.

Putting It All Together

Quilted by Diane Minkley

four square lap quilt

FINISHED BLOCK SIZE: 12″ × 12″ ■ FINISHED LAP QUILT: 64½″ × 88½″

The classic color combination of black and tan gives this quilt its timeless appeal. Large blocks cut into quarters and then pieced back together make this quilt look much more complicated than it really is!

materials

- 1½ yards total assorted blacks for pieced blocks and pieced border
- 1¾ yards total assorted browns for pieced blocks and pieced border
- 1¼ yards total assorted golds for pieced blocks
- 3¼ yards total assorted tans for pieced blocks
- 5⅞ yards for backing and binding
- 69″ × 93″ batting

cutting

Cut from the assorted blacks:

35 squares 5″ × 5″ for the pieced blocks

74 squares 2½″ × 2½″ for the pieced border

Cut from the assorted browns:

36 rectangles 2½″ × 5″ for the pieced blocks

36 rectangles 2½″ × 9″ for the pieced blocks

74 squares 2½″ × 2½″ for the pieced border

Cut from the assorted golds for the pieced blocks:

34 rectangles 2½″ × 5″

34 rectangles 2½″ × 9″

Cut from the assorted tans for the pieced blocks:

70 rectangles 2½″ × 9″

70 rectangles 2½″ × 13″

piecing

1. Piece the block as shown. Press. Make 35 blocks.

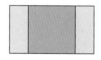

Step 1

Step 2

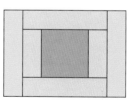

Step 3

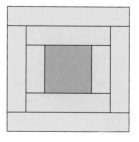

Step 4

2. Cut the pieced blocks into quarters, each measuring 6½″ × 6½″. Cut 140 quarters.

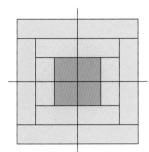

Cut blocks into quarters.

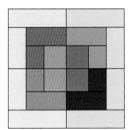

Sew quarters into blocks. Press. Make 35 blocks.

putting it all together

QUILT CENTER

1. Arrange and sew together the blocks in 7 rows of 5 blocks each. Press.

2. Sew together the rows to form the pieced block section of the quilt top. Press.

PIECED BORDER

1. Arrange and sew together 2 rows of 42 squares 2½″ × 2½″ from the assorted black and brown squares to make the side borders. Press.

2. Sew the 2 side borders to the quilt top. Press toward the border.

3. Arrange and sew together 2 rows of 32 squares 2½″ × 2½″ from the assorted blacks and browns to make the top and bottom borders. Press.

4. Sew the top and bottom borders to the quilt top. Press toward the border.

finishing

1. Layer the quilt top with batting and backing. Baste or pin.

2. Quilt as desired and bind.

Putting It All Together

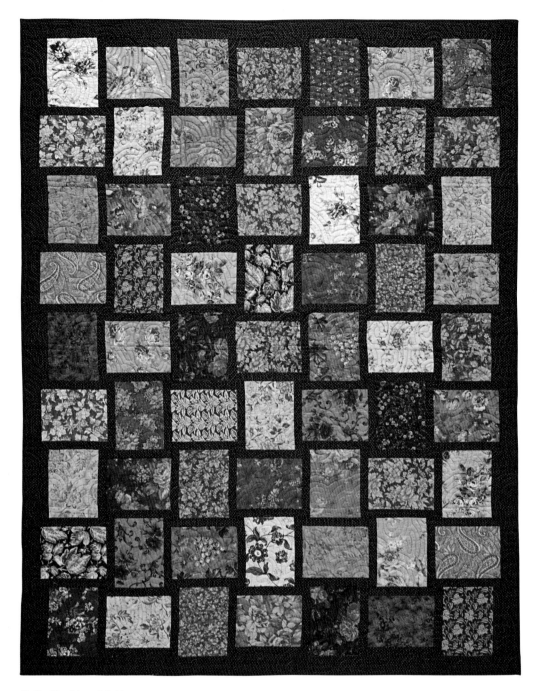

Quilted by Diane Minkley

carousel lap quilt

FINISHED BLOCK SIZE: 8″ × 8″ ■ **FINISHED LAP QUILT:** 60½″ × 76½″

This is a great quilt to showcase your favorite, fabulous large-scale prints. The cutting and piecing are fast and easy, making this a good choice if you are a beginning quiltmaker.

materials

- ¼ yard each of 32 different large prints for blocks
- 2¼ yards gray for lattice and borders
- 5¼ yards for backing and binding
- 65″ × 81″ batting

cutting

Cut 63 rectangles 6½″ × 8½″ from the assorted large prints for the blocks.

Cut from the gray:

  116 rectangles 1½″ × 8½″ for the lattice pieces

  10 rectangles 3½″ × 8½″ for the end lattice pieces in A rows

  8 rectangles 2½″ × 8½″ for the end lattice pieces in B rows

  2 strips 2½″ × 60½″ for the top and bottom borders*

  Cut 4 strips 2½″ × fabric width, piece end to end (see page 9), and cut the border strips.

piecing

1. Sew 2 lattice pieces 1½″ × 8½″ to the long sides of a large print rectangle to piece the block. Press. Make 31 blocks.

Make 31.

2. Arrange and sew together 3 blocks, 4 large print rectangles, and 6 lattice pieces 1½″ × 8½″ in a row. Add 3½″ × 8½″ lattice pieces to the ends. Press. Make 5 rows.

Pieced row A; make 5.

3. Arrange and sew together 4 blocks, 3 large print rectangles, and 6 lattice pieces 1½″ × 8½″ in a row. Add 2½″ × 8½″ lattice pieces to the ends. Press. Make 4 rows.

Pieced row B; make 4.

putting it all together

QUILT CENTER

Arrange and sew together the rows, alternating A rows and B rows. Press.

BORDER

Sew the top and bottom borders to the quilt top. Press.

finishing

1. Layer the quilt top with batting and backing. Baste or pin.

2. Quilt as desired and bind.

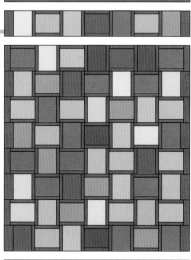

Putting It All Together

Quilted by Diane Minkley

tic-tac wall quilt

FINISHED BLOCK SIZE: 10″ × 10″ ■ **FINISHED WALL QUILT:** 50½″ × 50½″

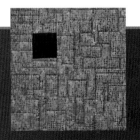

Brighten any room with this graphic wall quilt with a contemporary twist. Super simple cutting and piecing make this quilt go together quickly and easily. This is a great project for beginning quilters.

materials

- ¼ yard black for pieced blocks
- 2½ yards total assorted brights for pieced blocks
- 3½ yards for backing and binding
- 54″ × 54″ batting

cutting

Cut 25 squares 2½″ × 2½″ from the black for the pieced blocks.

Cut from the assorted brights for the pieced blocks:

25 squares 2½″ × 2½″

25 rectangles 2½″ × 6½″

25 rectangles 2½″ × 10½″

25 rectangles 6½″ × 10½″

piecing

1. Piece the block as shown. Press. Make 19 blocks.

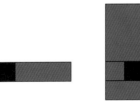

Step 1　　　　Step 2

2. Piece the block as shown. Press. Make 6 blocks.

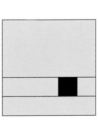

Step 1　　　　Step 2

putting it all together

1. Arrange and sew together the blocks in 5 rows of 5 blocks each. Press.

2. Sew together the rows to form the quilt top.

finishing

1. Layer the quilt top with batting and backing. Baste or pin.

2. Quilt as desired and bind.

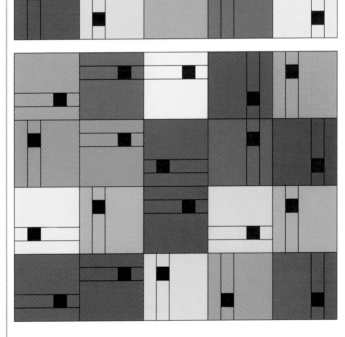

Putting It All Together

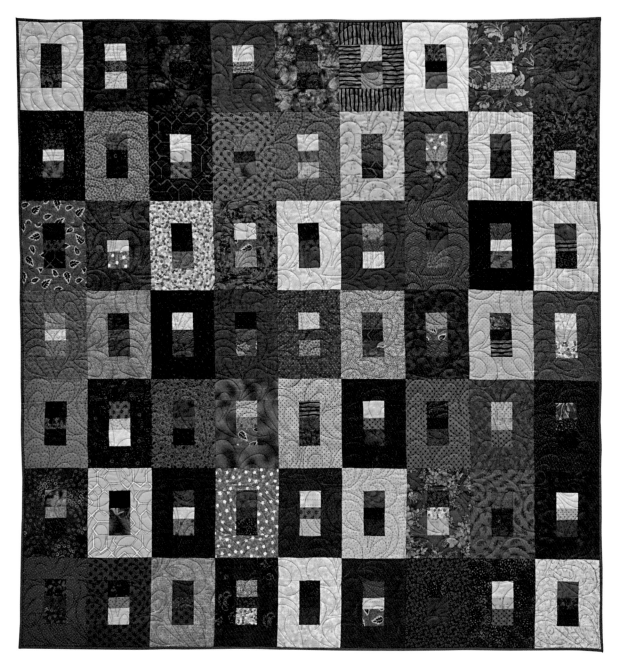

Quilted by Diane Minkley

mint chocolate wall quilt

FINISHED BLOCK SIZE: 6″ × 8″ ■ **FINISHED WALL QUILT:** 54½″ × 56½″

Rich, chocolate browns and minty, tealy greens
make this contemporary quilt simply delicious.

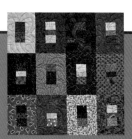

materials

- 2 yards total assorted teals for pieced blocks
- 2 yards total assorted browns for pieced blocks
- 3⅞ yards for backing and binding
- 58″ × 60″ batting

cutting

Cut from the assorted teals for the pieced blocks:

31 rectangles 2½″ × 1½″

62 rectangles 2½″ × 2″

64 rectangles 2½″ × 4½″

64 rectangles 2½″ × 6½″

Cut from the assorted browns for the pieced blocks:

32 rectangles 2½″ × 1½″

64 rectangles 2½″ × 2″

62 rectangles 2½″ × 4½″

62 rectangles 2½″ × 6½″

piecing

1. Piece the block as shown. Press. Make 32 teal blocks.

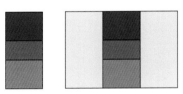

Step 1   Step 2

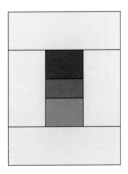

Step 3

2. Piece the block as shown. Make 31 brown blocks.

Step 1   Step 2

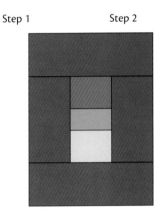

Step 3

putting it all together

1. Arrange and sew together the blocks in 7 rows of 9 blocks each. Press.

2. Sew together the rows to form the quilt top. Press.

finishing

1. Layer the quilt top with batting and backing. Baste or pin.

2. Quilt as desired and bind.

Putting It All Together

Quilted by Diane Minkley

bubble gum wall quilt

FINISHED BLOCK SIZE: 5″ × 5″ ■ FINISHED WALL QUILT: 53½″ × 53½″

Hand-dyed textured solids give this wall quilt its so soft suede look.

materials

- 2¾ yards total assorted brights for pieced blocks
- 1 yard indigo for lattice
- ¼ yard gray for lattice connecting squares
- 3¾ yards for backing and binding
- 57″ × 57″ batting

cutting

Cut 405 rectangles 1½″ × 5½″ from the assorted brights for the pieced blocks.

Cut 144 rectangles 1½″ × 5½″ from the indigo for the lattice.

Cut 64 squares 1½″ × 1½″ from the gray for the lattice connecting squares.

piecing

Sew together 5 rectangles 1½″ × 5½″ from the assorted brights to piece the block. Press. Make 81 blocks.

Pieced blocks; make 81.

putting it all together

1. Arrange the blocks in 9 rows of 9 blocks each, alternating the direction of the blocks.

2. Sew together 9 blocks and 8 lattice pieces in a row. Press. Make 9 rows.

3. Sew together 9 lattice pieces and 8 connecting squares in a row. Press. Make 8 rows.

Pieced lattice rows; make 8.

4. Sew together the block rows and lattice rows to form the quilt top. Press.

finishing

1. Layer the quilt top with batting and backing. Baste or pin.

2. Quilt as desired and bind.

Putting It All Together

Quilted by Diane Minkley

pop rocks wall quilt

FINISHED BLOCK SIZE: 8″ × 8″ ■ FINISHED WALL QUILT: 62½″ × 56½″

Rich jewel-toned fabrics make this quilt sparkle. The large-scale floral print used as a lattice gives the quilt its contemporary look.

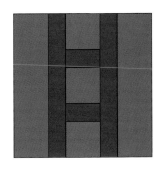

materials

- 2½ yards total assorted blues, purples, teals, reds, and greens for pieced blocks
- 2½ yards floral print for pieced blocks, lattice, and binding
- 3½ yards for backing
- 67" × 61" batting

cutting

Cut from the assorted blues, purples, teals, reds, and greens for the pieced blocks:

219 squares 2½" × 2½"

74 rectangles 2½" × 8½"

Cut from the floral print:

146 rectangles 1½" × 2½" for the pieced blocks

98 rectangles 1½" × 8½" for the pieced blocks

42 rectangles 1½" × 8½" for the lattice pieces

piecing

1. Piece block A as shown. Press. Make 25 blocks.

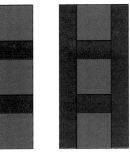

Step 1   Step 2

Step 3

2. Piece block B as shown. Press. Make 24 blocks.

Step 1

Step 2

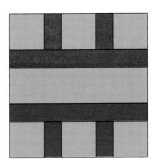

Step 3

putting it all together

1. Arrange the blocks in 7 rows of 7 blocks each, alternating the A blocks and B blocks.

2. Sew 7 blocks and 6 lattice pieces in a row. Press. Make 7 rows.

3. Sew together the rows to form the quilt top. Press.

finishing

1. Layer the quilt top with batting and backing. Baste or pin.

2. Quilt as desired and bind.

Putting It All Together

Quilted by Diane Minkley

blueberries and butterscotch wall quilt

FINISHED BLOCK SIZE: 10″ × 10″ ▪ FINISHED WALL QUILT: 58½″ × 58½″

The classic color combination of blue, brown, and tan gives this quilt a traditional flavor. Super simple cutting and piecing make this quilt quick and easy.

materials

- 2¼ yards total assorted lights for pieced blocks
- 1½ yards total assorted browns for pieced blocks and pieced borders
- ¾ yard total assorted blues for pieced blocks
- 4⅛ yards backing and binding
- 63″ × 63″ batting

cutting

Cut from the assorted lights for the pieced blocks:

65 rectangles 2½″ × 10½″

144 squares 2½″ × 2½″

Cut from the assorted browns:

52 squares 2½″ × 2½″ for the pieced blocks

108 rectangles 2½″ × 4½″ for the pieced border

Cut 104 squares 2½″ × 2½″ from the assorted blues for the pieced blocks.

piecing

1. Sew together 5 rectangles 2½″ × 10½″ from the assorted lights to piece the block. Press. Make 13 blocks.

Pieced blocks; make 13.

2. Sew together 5 rows of 5 squares 2½″ × 2½″ from the assorted lights and browns. Sew together the rows to piece the block. Press. Make 4 blocks.

Pieced blocks; make 4.

3. Sew together 5 rows of 5 squares 2½″ × 2½″ from the assorted lights and blues. Sew together the rows to piece the block. Press. Make 8 blocks.

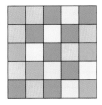

Pieced blocks; make 8.

putting it all together

QUILT CENTER

1. Arrange and sew together the blocks in 5 rows of 5 blocks each. Press.

2. Sew together the rows to form the quilt top. Press.

PIECED BORDER

1. Arrange and sew together 2 rows of 25 rectangles 2½″ × 4½″ from the assorted browns for the side borders. Press.

2. Sew the 2 side borders to the quilt top. Press toward the borders.

3. Arrange and sew together 2 rows of 29 rectangles 2½″ × 4½″ from the assorted browns for the top and bottom borders. Press.

4. Sew the top and bottom borders to the quilt top. Press toward the borders.

finishing

1. Layer the quilt top with batting and backing. Baste or pin.

2. Quilt as desired and bind.

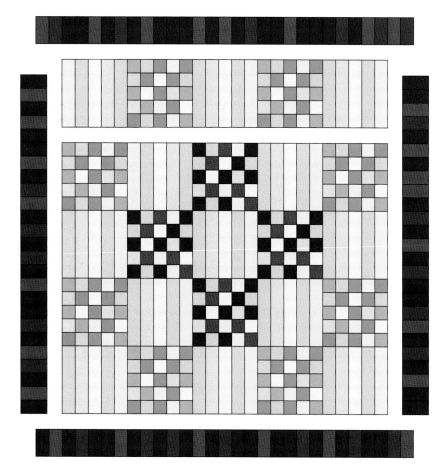

Putting It All Together

Quilted by Diane Minkley

going green table runner

FINISHED BLOCK SIZES: 10″ × 10″, 5″ × 5″ ■ FINISHED TABLE RUNNER: 20½″ × 60½″

Going green is easy when you whip up this table runner
from a smorgasbord of greens. This scrappy runner is sure
to brighten any tabletop.

materials

- 2 yards total assorted greens for pieced blocks and pieced border
- 2¼ yards for backing and binding
- 24″ × 64″ batting

cutting

Cut from the assorted greens for the pieced blocks:

5 squares 6½″ × 6½″

10 rectangles 1½″ × 6½″

20 rectangles 1½″ × 8½″

10 rectangles 1½″ × 10½″

Cut from the assorted greens for the pieced border blocks:

84 squares 1½″ × 1½″

112 rectangles 1½″ × 3½″

56 rectangles 1½″ × 5½″

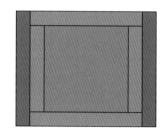

Step 3

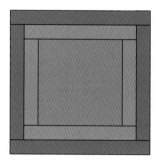

Step 4

piecing

1. Piece the block as shown. Press. Make 5 blocks.

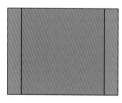

Step 1

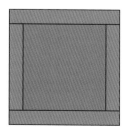

Step 2

2. Piece the border block as shown. Press. Make 28 blocks.

Step 1

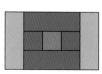

Step 2

Step 3

Step 4

putting it all together

1. Arrange and sew together 5 blocks to form the center of the table runner. Press.

2. Arrange and sew together 2 rows of 10 border blocks to make the side borders. Press.

3. Sew the 2 side borders to the runner top. Press toward the borders.

4. Arrange and sew together 2 rows of 4 border blocks to make the end borders. Press.

5. Sew the 2 end borders to the runner top. Press toward the borders.

finishing

1. Layer the table runner top with batting and backing. Baste or pin.

2. Quilt as desired and bind.

Putting It All Together

Quilted by Diane Minkley

rainbow twist table runner

FINISHED BLOCK SIZE: 5″ × 5″ ■ **FINISHED TABLE RUNNER:** 15½″ × 40½″

Brighten your tabletop with this framed,
square table runner. Fun and easy!

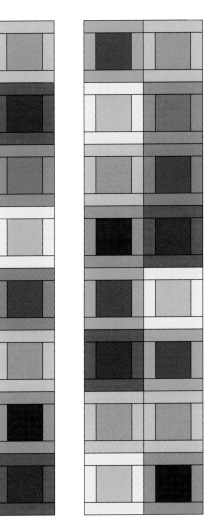

materials

- 1 yard total assorted brights for pieced blocks
- 1½ yards for backing and binding
- 19″ × 44″ batting

cutting

Cut from the assorted brights for the pieced blocks:

24 squares 3½″ × 3½″

48 rectangles 1½″ × 3½″

48 rectangles 1½″ × 5½″

piecing

Piece the block as shown. Press. Make 24 blocks.

Step 1

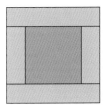

Step 2

putting it all together

1. Arrange and sew together the blocks in 3 rows of 8 blocks each. Press.

2. Sew together the rows to form the runner top. Press.

finishing

1. Layer the table runner top with batting and backing. Baste or pin.

2. Quilt as desired and bind.

Putting It All Together

Quilted by Diane Minkley

vanilla crème table runner

FINISHED BLOCK SIZE: 8″ × 8″ ■ **FINISHED TABLE RUNNER:** 20½″ × 44½″

Grace your table with this elegant runner pieced
with classic neutral fabrics. Simple and classy!

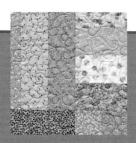

materials

- 1¼ yards total assorted neutrals for pieced blocks and pieced borders
- 1¾ yards for backing and binding
- 28" × 48" batting

cutting

Cut from the assorted neutrals:

40 rectangles 2½" × 8½" for the pieced blocks

60 squares 2½" × 2½" for the pieced borders

piecing

Sew together 4 rectangles 2½" × 8½" to piece the block. Press. Make 10 blocks.

Pieced blocks; make 10.

putting it all together

QUILT CENTER

1. Arrange and sew together the blocks in 2 rows of 5 blocks each. Press.

2. Sew together the rows. Press.

PIECED BORDER

1. Arrange and sew together 2 rows of 20 squares 2½" × 2½" to make the side borders. Press.

2. Sew the 2 side borders to the runner top. Press.

3. Arrange and sew together 2 rows of 10 squares 2½" × 2½" to make the end borders. Press.

4. Sew the 2 end borders to the runner top. Press.

finishing

1. Layer the table runner top with batting and backing. Baste or pin.

2. Quilt as desired and bind.

Putting It All Together

Quilted by Diane Minkley

color splash table runner

FINISHED BLOCK SIZE: 10" × 10" ■ **FINISHED TABLE RUNNER:** 16½" × 56½"

Large-scale contemporary prints will add a splash
of color to your table. Vibrant and exciting!

materials

- ⅓ yard each of 5 different large-scale prints for pieced blocks
- ½ yard coordinating print for pieced blocks and outer border
- ¼ yard contrasting print for inner border
- 2 yards for backing and binding
- 20″ × 60″ batting

cutting

Cut from the assorted large-scale prints for the pieced blocks:

    5 squares 2½″ × 2½″

    5 rectangles 2½″ × 6½″

    5 rectangles 2½″ × 10½″

    5 rectangles 6½″ × 10½″

Cut from the coordinating print:

    5 squares 2½″ × 2½″ for the pieced blocks

    2 strips 2½″ × 52½″ for the side outer borders

    2 strips 2½″ × 16½″ for the end outer borders

    Cut 3 strips 2½″ x fabric width, piece the strips end to end (see page 9), and cut the border strips.

Cut from the contrasting print:

    2 strips 1½″ × 50½″ for the side inner borders

    2 strips 1½″ × 12½″ for the end inner borders

    Cut 3 strips 1½″ x fabric width, piece the strips end to end (see page 9), and cut the border strips.

piecing

1. Piece the block as shown. Make 4 blocks.

Step 1

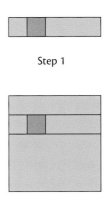

Step 2

2. Piece the block as shown. Make 1 block.

Step 1

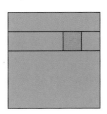

Step 2

putting it all together

TABLE RUNNER CENTER

Arrange and sew together 5 blocks to form the center of the table runner. Press.

INNER BORDER

1. Sew the side inner borders to the runner top. Press toward the borders.

2. Sew the end inner borders to the runner top. Press toward the borders.

OUTER BORDER

1. Sew the side outer borders to the runner top. Press toward the borders.

2. Sew the end outer borders to the runner top. Press toward the borders.

finishing

1. Layer the table runner top with batting and backing. Baste or pin.

2. Quilt as desired and bind.

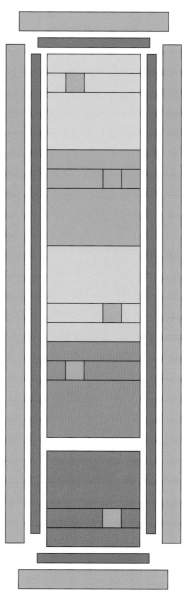

Putting It All Together

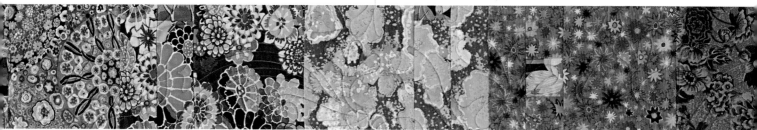

Quilted by Diane Minkley

pastel picnic table runner

FINISHED BLOCK SIZE: 10″ × 10″ ■ FINISHED TABLE RUNNER: 14½″ × 54½″

Soft pastels make up this easy table runner.
Fresh and easy—great for spring!

materials

- ¾ yard total assorted lights for pieced blocks
- ⅜ yard total assorted oranges, yellows, and pinks for pieced blocks
- ⅜ yard total assorted teals and greens for pieced border
- 2 yards for backing and binding
- 18" × 58" batting

cutting

Cut from the assorted lights for the pieced blocks:

    10 rectangles 2½" × 10½"

    36 squares 2½" × 2½"

Cut 39 squares 2½" × 2½" from the assorted oranges, yellows, and pinks for the pieced blocks.

Cut 64 squares 2½" × 2½" from the assorted teals and greens for the pieced border.

piecing

1. Sew together 5 rectangles 2½" × 10½" from the assorted lights to piece the block. Press. Make 2 blocks.

Pieced blocks; make 2.

2. Sew together 5 rows of 5 squares 2½" × 2½" from the assorted lights, oranges, yellows, or pinks. Sew together the rows to piece the block.

Press. Make 3 blocks.

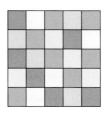

Pieced blocks; make 3.

putting it all together

TABLE RUNNER CENTER

Arrange and sew together 5 blocks to form the runner top. Press.

PIECED BORDER

1. Arrange and sew together 2 rows of 25 squares 2½" × 2½" from the assorted teals and greens to make the side borders. Press.

2. Sew the side borders to the runner top. Press toward the borders.

3. Arrange and sew together 2 rows of 7 squares 2½" × 2½" from the assorted teals and greens to make the end borders. Press.

4. Sew the end borders to the runner top. Press toward the borders.

finishing

1. Layer the table runner top with batting and backing. Baste or pin.

2. Quilt as desired and bind.

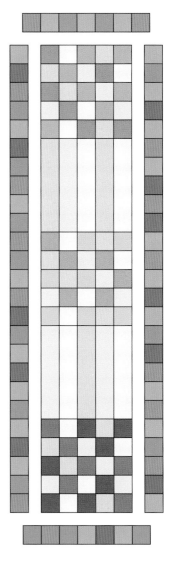

Putting It All Together

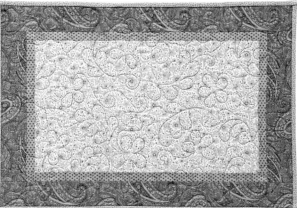

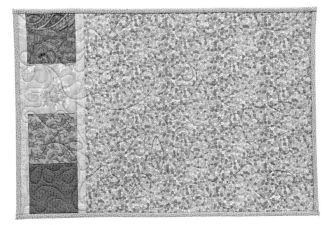

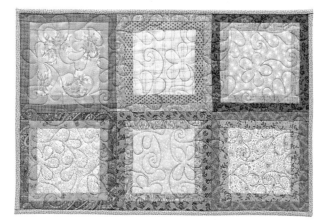

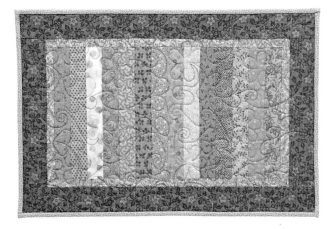

placemats

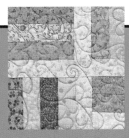

Mix and match a set of placemats for yourself or to give as a gift to someone special. There are six different designs to choose from. I used a variety of neutrals, which look stunning on a dark table. However, the placemats will look great no matter what palette you choose.

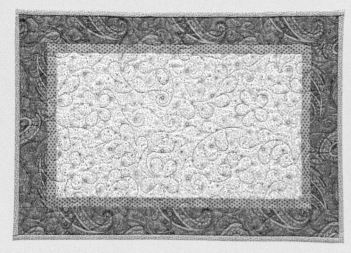

plain and simple placemat

FINISHED PLACEMAT: 18½" × 12½"

materials

- ⅓ yard light print for center
- ⅛ yard light tan for inner border
- ¼ yard tan paisley for outer border
- ¾ yard for backing and binding
- 16" × 22" batting

cutting

Cut 1 rectangle 14½" × 8½" from the light print for the placemat center.

Cut from the light tan:

2 strips 1" × 8½" for the side inner borders

2 strips 1" × 15½" for the top and bottom inner borders

Cut from the tan paisley:

2 strips 2" × 9½" for the side outer borders

2 strips 2" × 18½" for the top and bottom outer borders

putting it all together

1. Sew the 2 side inner borders to the placemat. Press toward the borders.

2. Sew the top and bottom inner borders to the placemat. Press toward the borders.

3. Sew the 2 side outer borders to the placemat. Press toward the borders.

4. Sew the top and bottom outer borders to the placemat. Press toward the borders.

finishing

1. Layer the placemat with batting and backing. Baste or pin.

2. Quilt as desired and bind.

Putting It All Together

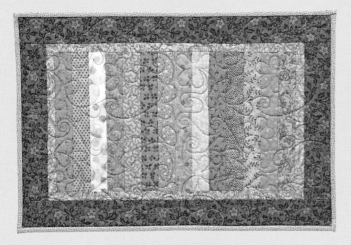

zippy strippy placemat

FINISHED PLACEMAT: 18½″ × 12½″

Quilted by Diane Minkley

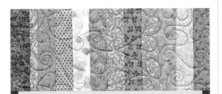

materials

- ¼ yard total assorted neutrals for center
- ⅛ yard light tan for inner border
- ¼ yard dark tan for outer border
- ¾ yard backing and binding
- 16″ × 22″ batting

cutting

Cut 14 strips 1½″ × 8½″ from the assorted neutrals for the placemat center.

Cut from the light tan:

2 strips 1″ × 8½″ for the side inner borders

2 strips 1″ × 15½″ for the top and bottom inner borders

Cut from the dark tan:

2 strips 2″ × 9½″ for the side outer borders

2 strips 2″ × 18½″ for the top and bottom outer borders

piecing

Sew together 14 rectangles 1½″ × 8½″ from the assorted neutrals to form the placemat center. Press.

putting it all together

1. Sew the 2 side inner borders to the placemat. Press toward the borders.

2. Sew the top and bottom inner borders to the placemat. Press toward the borders.

3. Sew the 2 side outer borders to the placemat. Press toward the borders.

4. Sew the top and bottom outer borders to the placemat. Press toward the borders.

finishing

1. Layer the placemat with batting and backing. Baste or pin.

2. Quilt as desired and bind.

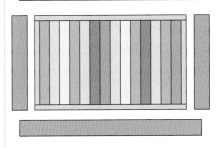

Putting It All Together

square-in-a-square placemat

FINISHED PLACEMAT: 18½" × 12½"

Quilted by Diane Minkley

materials

- ½ yard total assorted neutrals for pieced blocks
- ¾ yard backing and binding
- 16" × 22" batting

cutting

Cut from the assorted neutrals for the pieced blocks:

24 squares 2½" × 2½"

48 rectangles 1" × 2½"

48 rectangles 1" × 3½"

piecing

Piece the block as shown. Press. Make 24 blocks.

Step 1

Step 2

putting it all together

1. Arrange and sew together 4 rows of 6 blocks each. Press.

2. Sew together the rows to form the placemat. Press.

finishing

1. Layer the placemat with batting and backing. Baste or pin.

2. Quilt as desired and bind.

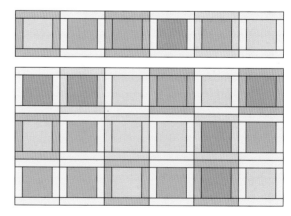

Putting It All Together

six square placemat

FINISHED PLACEMAT: 18½" × 12½"

Quilted by Diane Minkley

materials

- ½ yard total assorted neutrals for pieced blocks
- ¾ yard backing and binding
- 16" × 22" batting

cutting

Cut from the assorted neutrals for the pieced blocks:

    6 squares 4½" × 4½"

    12 rectangles 1" × 4½"

    24 rectangles 1" × 5½"

    12 rectangles 1" × 6½"

piecing

Piece the block as shown. Press. Make 6 blocks.

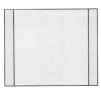

Step 1

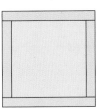

Step 2

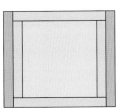

Step 3

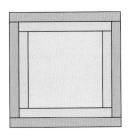

Step 4

putting it all together

1. Arrange and sew together 2 rows of 3 blocks each. Press.

2. Sew together the rows to form the placemat. Press.

finishing

1. Layer the placemat with batting and backing. Baste or pin.

2. Quilt as desired and bind.

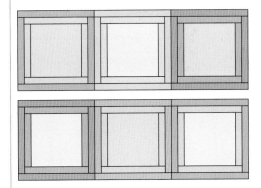

Putting It All Together

striped squares placemat

FINISHED PLACEMAT: 18½" × 12½"

Quilted by Diane Minkley

materials

- ⅓ yard total assorted neutrals for pieced blocks
- ¼ light tan for lattice and border
- ¾ yard backing and binding
- 16" × 22" batting

cutting

Cut 30 rectangles 1½" × 5½" from the assorted neutrals for the pieced blocks.

Cut from the light tan:

    4 rectangles 1½" × 5½" for the lattice

    1 strip 1½" × 17½" for the lattice

    2 strips 1" × 11½" for the side borders

    2 strips 1" × 18½" for the top and bottom borders

piecing

Sew together 5 rectangles 1½" × 5½" from the assorted neutrals to piece the block. Press. Make 6 blocks.

Pieced block; make 6.

putting it all together

1. Arrange the blocks into 2 rows of 3 blocks each.

2. Sew together 3 blocks and 2 lattice pieces 1½" × 5½" in a row. Press. Make 2 rows.

3. Sew together the rows and the lattice pieces 1½" × 17½" to form the placemat center. Press.

4. Sew the 2 side borders to the placemat top. Press toward the borders.

5. Sew the top and bottom borders to the placemat top. Press toward the borders.

finishing

1. Layer the placemat with batting and backing. Baste or pin.

2. Quilt as desired and bind.

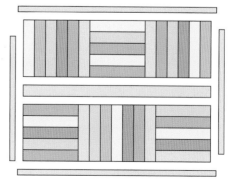

Putting It All Together

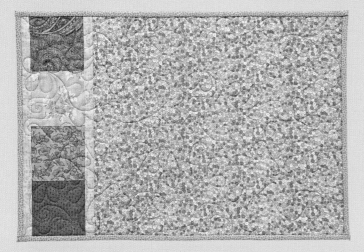

side stripe placemat

FINISHED PLACEMAT: 18½″ × 12½″

materials

- ½ yard light tan for center
- ¼ yard total assorted neutrals for pieced stripe and lattice
- ¾ yard backing and binding
- 16″ × 22″ batting

cutting

Cut 1 rectangle 14½″ × 12½″ from the light tan for the center.

Cut from the assorted neutrals:

  4 squares 3½″ × 3½″ for the pieced stripe

  2 strips 1″ × 12½″ for the lattice

putting it all together

1. Sew together 4 squares 3½″ × 3½″ from assorted neutrals in a row. Press.

2. Sew the lattice pieces to each side of the pieced row. Press.

3. Sew the pieced row to the placemat rectangle. Press.

finishing

1. Layer the placemat with batting and backing. Baste or pin.

2. Quilt as desired and bind.

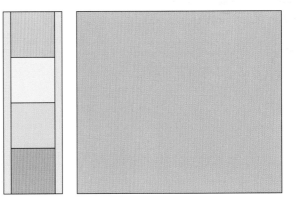

Putting It All Together

about the author

Kim Schaefer is from southeastern Wisconsin, where she lives with her husband, Gary; her sons, Sam and Gator; and her dog, Rio. Kim and Gary also have two daughters, Cody and Ali, and two college-bound sons, Max and Ben. Kim has two stepdaughters, Danielle and Tina, and two stepsons, Gary Jr. and Dax.

Kim began sewing at an early age, which she says was a nightmare for her mom, who continually and patiently untangled bobbin messes. Kim was formally educated at the University of Wisconsin in Milwaukee, where she studied fine arts and majored in fiber. At age 23, Kim took her first quilting class and was immediately hooked.

In 1996, Little Quilt Company made its debut at Quilt Market in Minneapolis. In addition to designing quilt patterns, Kim designs fabric for Andover/Makower and works with Leo Licensing, who licenses her designs for nonfabric products.

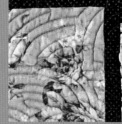

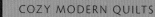

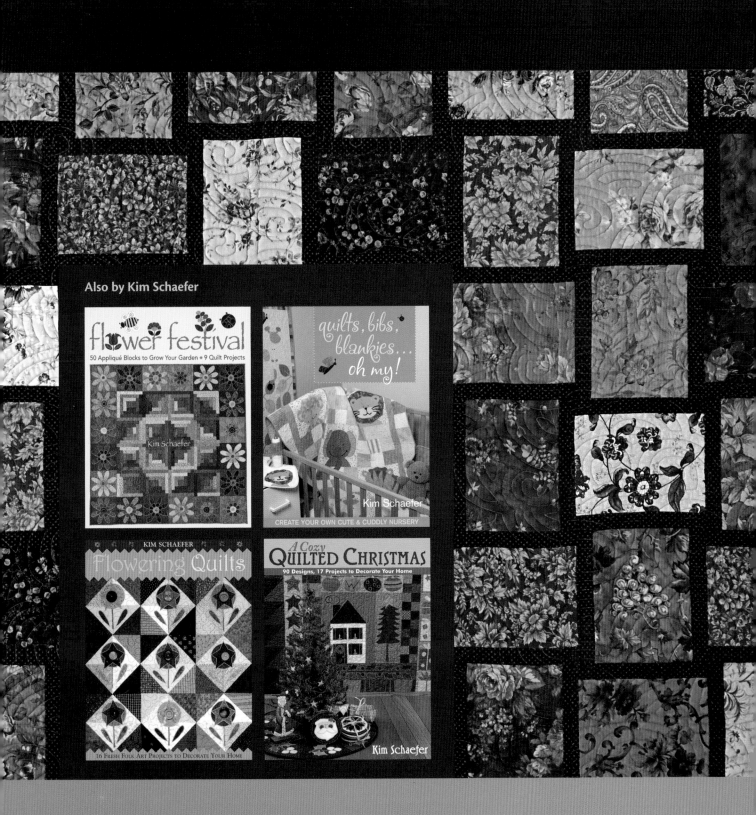

Also by Kim Schaefer

flower festival
50 Appliqué Blocks to Grow Your Garden • 9 Quilt Projects
Kim Schaefer

quilts, bibs, blankies... oh my!
Kim Schaefer
CREATE YOUR OWN CUTE & CUDDLY NURSERY

KIM SCHAEFER
Flowering Quilts
16 Fresh Folk Art Projects to Decorate Your Home

A Cozy QUILTED CHRISTMAS
90 Designs, 17 Projects to Decorate Your Home
Kim Schaefer

Great Titles *from* C&T PUBLISHING

Available at your local retailer or **www.ctpub.com** *or* **800.284.1114**

For a list of other fine books from C&T Publishing,
ask for a free catalog:

C&T PUBLISHING, INC.

P.O. Box 1456
Lafayette, CA 94549
(800) 284-1114

Email: ctinfo@ctpub.com
Website: www.ctpub.com

Tips and Techniques can be found at www.ctpub.com > Consumer
Resources > Quiltmaking Basics: Tips & Techniques for Quiltmaking
& More

C&T Publishing's professional photography services are now available
to the public. Visit us at www.ctmediaservices.com.

For quilting supplies:

COTTON PATCH

1025 Brown Ave.
Lafayette, CA 94549
Store: (925) 284-1177
Mail order: (925) 283-7883

Email: CottonPa@aol.com
Website: www.quiltusa.com

Note: Fabrics used in the quilts shown may not be currently
available, as fabric manufacturers keep most fabrics in
print for only a short time.